Leaf-dappled Light

Rodney Purvis

Leaf-dappled Light
Collected Poems 1969–2020

Acknowledgements

Several of these poems have appeared in other publications.

'In a Smoking Compartment', 'Meditation on the Death of W.H.Auden', 'On Seeing a Wallaby South of Eildon', 'Hiatus' and 'Lines on a Picture of a Lady' appeared in *Nation Review*.

'Au Musée des Beaux', 'Ezra Pound in London', 'Ezra Pound at Pisa', 'A Day in a Life', 'Impressions of Murndal', 'Compound Failure', 'Proceedings', 'Zoo Images', 'Alternate Sundays', 'Resurrection', 'Portrait of a Tenant', 'Night on Mt Erica', 'Life-drawing Model', 'Poetess meets Poet', 'Woman Sea and Myth' and 'Hamlet in Suburbia' appeared in *Quadrant*.

'Refugees' was published in *Prospect*.

This book is dedicated to
my wife Sophie
and daughter Melissa
for their love and support.

Leaf-dappled Light: Collected Poems 1969–2020
ISBN 978 1 76109 352 4
Copyright © text Rodney Purvis 2022
Cover image: Melissa Teng-Purvis

First published 2022 by
GINNINDERRA PRESS
PO Box 3461 Port Adelaide 5015 Australia
www.ginninderrapress.com.au

Contents

In a Smoking Compartment	7
Meditation on the Death of W.H. Auden	8
On Seeing a Wallaby South of Eildon	9
Hiatus	10
My Cathedral	11
Lines on a Picture of a Lady	13
Au Musée Des Beaux Arts	14
Ezra Pound in London	15
Ezra Pound at Pisa	16
A Day in a Life	17
Impressions of Murndal	19
Compound Failure	21
Proceedings	22
Zoo Images	23
Alternate Sundays	26
Resurrection	28
Portrait of a Tenant	30
Night on Mt Erica	32
Life-drawing Model	34
Poetess Meets Poet	35
Hamlet in Suburbia	36
Refugees	37
The Outsider	38
Odalisque	41
The Minoans	43
Leaves	45
Rough-edged Voices	46
Out of the Clamour	48
Last Year at Marienbad	49
Suburban Adieux	50

Lines on a Photo of Bob Dylan, c. 1966	51
On the Death of Anna Magdalena Bach	52
Woman, Sea and Myth	53
Storm After Calm	54
Burke and Wills at Cooper Creek	55
Meditation on the Past while Swimming: A Tale of Two Countries	57
Song for Miriam	59
Ballade	61
Bibliomaiden	62
Marine Vignette	64
Thoughts of an Educator	65
By the Pool: A Summer Poem	66
A Cinnamon Girl in Cosmos Book Store	67
Cricket Ground, Walhalla	68
Bob Dylan at Budokan	69
Viewing John Olsen's Pictures at the National Gallery of Victoria	70
Varykino Lost	72
Muirstead	74
Candle in the Wind	77
Your Gypsy Dress	78

In a Smoking Compartment

A train.
Men enter, slump and grope
For seats and cigarettes.
A girl bent double,
Tickles the contents of her dolly-bag,
Secures a fag
And settles down to a blue, smoke haze.

Papers rustle;
Wrestled with, are folded, read:
FRANCE RAMPART IN THE PACIFIC!*
Screech banner headlines spread
As the train lurches,
Snakes, then locks
To tumble down a cutting.

A gentleman, romantic in attire,
No doubt of intellectual pretension,
Sits neatly clothed in condescension;
Quietly tendering a Gaulois fire.

Subscribers to indigenous weed,
Aware of emanations which intrude
Beyond the bounds of civil decency,
Knit nervous brows in introverted consternation
And conclude,
As to what falls out
In this careering compartment,
You can't help but count down
Your fellow traveller.

* This was written when the French were testing atomic weapons in the Pacific, in the 1970s.

Meditation on the Death of W.H. Auden

The tributes have been written,
The obituaries rendered. The notices
Noticed; the rituals attended. Immortality,
Guaranteed sometime ago, is finally
Conferred. Catalogued
And ranged on library shelves,
His works assume that timeless look.

Eliot, Auden, Pound.
In the darkness of this age's auditorium
The footlights flicker
On each exit. We have seen
Their departures. The great ones have exceeded us
A little more irretrievably this time.

Ordinary men may leave
A family or a business enterprise.
Some more successful may bequeath
A public monument, a scandal
Or a political stratagem.
The poet when he dies leaves orders
That the stone remain
Perpetually rolled backward from the tomb.
We appropriate the relics:
He is resurrected
Through some fated womb.

On Seeing a Wallaby South of Eildon

Dusk. At the next bend I see him,
Silhouetted blue-black
Under a drooping eucalypt. He sees
I keep on coming. Nerves,
Suspended in their tension,
Snap: he breaks
For the bushes, thuds the forest ferns.
He knew the blackman's furtiveness
And absence; the reality
Of the sudden, darted shaft,
The brief death agony, oblivion:
Part of the natural order.

When Cook brought men and guns,
The animal learnt a new game:
The blackman's darted shaft became
A metal death-stick belching flame.

Now man and beast can never meet
Upon a mountain track, but that
Two hundred years of apprehended fear
Beat up within the animal's blood-cautioned memory.
The same larrikin hand that slights this countryside
With beer cans,
Pulls the trigger.

Hiatus

The red and green strips in the café door
Blow almost rigid in the summer wind.
The milk bar couple, vacant, stare
Out into the afternoon; the year
Is worked out, finished,
All accounts seem settled.

Small things irritate.
A cold wind blows despite a dazzling sun,
Lifts the newsprint page I'm reading,
Riffles the paper wrapping the food I'm eating.
The day is blue, bright, quiet
And restless: we await
The passing of this dying year's
Hiatus.

My Cathedral

Near Healesville, Victoria

Before you pass St Ronan's Well,* always spring-full,
The road is bordered on each side
By tall, white-grey streaked mountain ash rearing
Out of a lower storey of tree-ferns.
These prehistoric ferns enhance the forest's base,
Like nature's side altars, icons; finely verdured,
A strength and delicacy that endures
Heat, cold, fire and men's passing.

The giant columns arch up
Out of this verdant filigree and meet
High in the vaults of their upper stories,
A great, natural arch.

This my cathedral.
Not the cold interiors of institutional megaliths
With stone steps, arches, ceilings, hard stone floors;
Columns polished and sanded.
These man-made caverns of nominal religions
Do not hold this bushland mystery,
But are the residual artefacts of probity
Enshrining our ancestors' Victorian notions of service
In antipodean clones of Europe's churches.

---

* Saint Ronan was a Celtic saint born in Ireland probably in the sixth century AD. He embarked on a voyage to Brittany, where he set up a hermitage, practised an ascetic lifestyle and attracted many followers.

In these edifices, we sense no emotion
Printed on the air, no ambience;
Nothing truly numinous.
It is only among ferns and arching trees and forest green
That I feel the stirrings of devotion.

Lines on a Picture of a Lady

Body slung across the page; it seems
She is a woman out of dreams;

With head inclined in narcissistic gaze,
Her body shimmers in the morning haze:

This giant torso singing female grace
Floats free, outside, beyond the picture space.

Her right hand splayed beneath a sun-cusped breast,
Her left upon her downy belly rests

From dappled navel where the thumb is laid,
To rounded hip receding into shade:

So, knowingly she cups the bowl around.
Her hand suspended thus above the ground –

The fingers in didactic pose –
Incline the eye towards the lady's toes,

And in that line there lies the flickering crest,
Of all her body's parts this is the best:

Dark at the centre, russet round the edge,
Between the columns of her thighs, the sun-licked sedge.

Some men seek truth by ways abstruse, profound;
Yet here is truth, and life's real battleground.

Au Musée Des Beaux Arts

It was all right by the Delaunay,
But I began to feel you slipping
Away amongst the temporary exhibits
And in the hall of the Dutch Masters,
Dark amber shadows were drifting between us.
There was a fleeting impression
Of light and coherence
In front of the Monets,

But by the time we had come to the Greek vases,
I had lost you completely.

Ezra Pound in London

With *Tapers Quenched* but a mind on fire,
You came to London and you razed
That city's stolid and conventional towers.
Within days you knew everyone important,
Had blue-stockings swooning at your feet:
A literary lynx, stalking her halls and corridors.

Not everybody's cup of tea: bounding across the floor
Of a chophouse to give Aldington
The 'lowdown' on Sappho; the green baize
Trousers, pink coat, goatee,
Silver-topped cane, scoop of flame red hair,
The calculated *distrait* of the *poète maudit*.
One blue earring. Some found you 'amusing',
Others, 'not the thing'.

Generously, you took over Bill Yeats' soirees
Proffering his cigarettes, chianti, the bright fruits
Of your staccato genius. He didn't seem to mind
But others less genial envied your talent
And despised your bombast.
You were not always applauded.

Suddenly: stasis. No longer writing,
Finished with London. By your thirtieth year
You had founded a movement, created a language,
Had already met those of real interest; discovered
The important talents, set them into the current:
European Ezra, Yank exile, broadcaster…

Ezra Pound at Pisa

Locked up in Pisa by the Americans, like Nabonidis,
Like an animal in a steel cage, open
To the weather: dust, sun, wind, cold; all else
Barred to you.
Mercifully, conditions modified;
Privileges were granted: your gaolers –
Imprisoned men – discovered you were no criminal –
An eccentric maybe – but 'goddam, a likeable enough old
man' – with strange words falling from your lips.
And so you shadow-boxed, walked brisk circuits
Of the camp for exercise
And nights, back into your stride, you pounded
The camp's sole typewriter. Until, one evening,
Eyes narrowing, you knew
They had come for you. Calmly you closed the book
You were reading, smiled at the orderly,
Turned from the lamplight.
Clipped into handcuffs, they flew you back
To America. Brought before the courts,
They locked you up for ten years in St Elizabeth's,
But by then you were already a legend.

A Day in a Life

After a day of:
Year 10 History, where I try to explain
The niceties of the Hindu concept of asrama
To two groups of young people most of whom
Are not interested and fractious and silly
And sometimes just damned rude;
And year 9 English where I read *Echo and Narcissus*
And the period tails off into a minimal response
And in order to salvage it, I dash the usual
Chaos-averting comprehension questions
Onto the blackboard;
And Geography where a reasonably structured period
Concludes with an injunction to 'Complete this for homework!'
And after the faculty meetings and the noticeboards
And the milling students and the public address
System, and being bound to my desk like Prometheus
To his rock of pain,

I proceed to the New World supermarket,
Where in an atmosphere of sterilised, factitious calm,
The muzak over the loudspeakers, expressionless faces
Gliding above aluminium trolleys, the neatly packaged vegetables;
The bright red meat in its plastic wrappers,
I see a girl in a green and yellow tracksuit, flick a glance
My way briefly, as she passes on the other side
Of the cattle-race cash register queues –

And the mind's screen lights up to a table…
Whose this massed hair, sienna, enshadowed, on whose
Pale cheek this crimson lozenge printed,
On whose white throat this ruby pentangle
Cast by candlelight
Through burgundy-stained glass?

But at my back, a blue-smoked checkout chick picks up
The microphone and intones the usual litany,
'This store will close in two minutes
Will customers kindly complete their purchases and proceed…'
And I obediently proceed, dazed and disorientated
Out into a twilight of vacuity and small town ennui.

Impressions of Murndal

for Catherine

We should have come into that library
After a day's loose-limbed labour in the fields,
Hay-baling, tree-felling or driving
Sheep to new pasture.

I came cold-cringed, replete
With negativity into your valley:
Brick ochre, lime-green
Elms in white mist.

From an urban cottage, mind-dulling
Walks over the same pavements,
Moonlight on corrupted waters,
I had come to Murndal:

To a fire of massive logs, chairs of red leather.
Here it seemed natural
To forget rule of thumb, pouring
The yellow whisky into large glasses.

Thus feeling like a god, one could survey
The crow, the owl and parakeets
In the frozen aviary above the tiers
Of gold lettering on spines of sepia books.

Yet all this was forgotten when we came
Into the dining room of this stately home.
Oils in the English manner hung
In the gloom above us. A foundling lamb

Clattered the parquet floor; a white cat
Coiled in the serving trolley, arched
His mouth upward to the steaming roast. The bathroom
Was a suitable prelude to this grand salon:

Washbasin ten paces in a farther corner; shower
A soap's throw to the left; a damp towel hung
From one of six white pegs – elbow room.
I have always felt the need to live on a large scale.

Compound Failure

Solitary
At the end of a day half-tasted;
Sedentary in that place, a witness

To your coming, dark-eyed lady
In your long skirts of the Nineties,
Waist-length hair and your white
Aesthetic face.

Amid the detritus of the waning day,
My feckless glances, subtle as searchlight
Whipping your whiteness. There were no rivals –
Not ten paces of distance between us…

Intelligent lady, since you departed
Angry at such ministrations,
Know that you also have troubled me greatly;

That I sit, compounding initial failure
By failing to find you in words.

Proceedings

Strange to see you in that corridor of faces
Of clients and lawyers, heads bent in the haze
Of cigarette smoke, last minute consultations.
You looked so young. Perhaps it was the parting
Of your hair, or some old coat I'd known you were wearing.
This is not flattery, for it seemed that nothing
In these past twelve years had left a mark on you.
Almost as though in this cancelling of our liaison,
You had reverted to the woman you had been before
Our first meetings, when we had new love freshly known.
Our case was called, we entered you and I,
Taking the plush chairs, green and stainless steel
Behind our lawyers side by side in the back row.
Some brief formalities, and the cold
Iron hand of the law like a guillotine
Set us apart. I stole a sideways glance
Like newly-weds in life and movies – the crowd still moved
Outside, oblivious in the corridors – you let the moment go
Thus were we parted,
Mute spectators at our own dumb show.

Zoo Images

for Sophie

Mandrills and Baboons

The mandrill's brilliant mask, scarlet, Prussian blue,
Stares at us over the bent backs of dog-apes,
Engrossed in mutual grooming. Their buttocks bright crimson,
Grotesque contusions bulge from beneath them
Like swollen boles upon timber:
How nature expends such energy to incite copulation.

Baboons, a small group of heads –
Gimlet eyes set like slots into granite,
Regard us like a stand
Of Easter Island visages. We turn,

Walk only a few paces – sudden explosion
Of shrill baboon barks, simian screams:
The mandrill now on all fours, a streak of blurred colour
Scatters the groomers, shreds the cage into sunlight and shadow.

Giraffes

The giraffes move close to us, elegant, gracile,
Over the brown dust of their enclosure
With the slow gravity of sea horses,
Or sea plants beneath water.

One sways its neck up to the young leaf tips
The grey, wet tongue protrudes languidly
With the accuracy of a humming bird's
Probing for nectar.

Their necks and limbs are out of all proportion,
Effete, attenuated horses, living follies;
They are themselves the end tips
Of some dead branch of evolution.

Black Gibbon

We view the black gibbon from high up, behind glass;
The enclosure is a brush-lined space not ten feet square,
Fractured by a sculpture of white boughs.
At first, he just hangs there from long, loose arms:
Not much happening.
He is no chirruping marmoset, but a glossy, hirsute chap
Whose size and elasticity attract the eye.

Suddenly, he slings the torpor off, himself
Around the circumference of branches, loosely, slowly –
Then he hots it up, doubles the pace, passing softly
Round and through the branches' filigree.
He swings for the pure joy of it,
He swings as we are breathing.
His attitude's detached, insouciant, though never proud.
There seems no possibility of error,
This is not done by logic;
His being is not violated by thought.

He circuits round these clean, white boughs
Like some small, powerful planet
Whose course is set for it.
He is on the glass's other side:
We cannot touch him.

At Melbourne Zoological Gardens

Alternate Sundays

It's the older one that worries me the most, the girl, first born –
The boy too young to know the turbulence,
Tattered ribbon-ends ripped fabric
Of the doomed relationship – but she was there
And I pray she was not touched or marked by it…
So it's she, when I pick them up alternate Sundays,
Meets me undemonstratively at the door I knock on,
Barely offering her cheek to kiss, turned away
A little, she sits beside me as we take the same road
Back to my place, gazes dumbly from the window,
Is monosyllabic in reply
To questions posed to pry her week's account –
Reminding me of my own adolescent dull reluctance
For response my parents tried to rouse in me.
But later, an hour into the visit and she thaws,
Comes little mother, staggering around the flat
With Lissa babe in arms; she wants to play at chasings –
A game I'm bad at being chased –
Then when I least expect it, when in company,
And talking to some friends, she sidles up
And slips onto my lap, seeks contact, cuddles…
And I slide
Back to the two of them upon that platform, sliding
Back from me, leaving – why was I always leaving
A good wife and babe in arms? And what force captured me
And drew me out and down that line? If God exists He knows
This heart that's tugged at by the memory
Down into the turbid waters of the past.

Tugged then, drawn out and down
By the black shark ego and identity,
Till heart's reel spent, too taut,
The fragile fabric of the marriage fraught;
Was rent, the lines were snagged and snapped.
Such dark reflections, and the mind can't stay
Stranded on these darker shoals of time, but slithers off
To float back up again to find itself
Bobbing in the present's light and noise and bubbly childrens' speech
And Flora on my knee, slips off, runs calling to her brother,
'Come on, Daddy, catch me!'

Resurrection

after Piero della Francesca

It is so easy to forget, so easy to lapse
Into the sleep the soldiery indulge in
At the picture's base.

All men of pleasant mien, all ordinary men you'd see
A beer in hand or shooting pool
In any bar room. All well-proportioned men,
Handsome in hose and breast-plate.

While He, awakened, resolute, stands
One foot planted on the conquered catafalque;
Solitary, banner-bearing, flat-stomached in purple robes,
An effulgent aura about his uncompromising head.

Behind, the Galilean trees echo
His legend and His uprightness:
Those on the left have barren crowns of thorns,
Those on the right are green in new fecundity.

The sleeping soldiery answer in their shapes
The straggling bushes and the passive hills;
The random thickets and the sleeping stones:
The quiescence of this barren wilderness.

Why does He rise so self-possessed above them,
Why should they sleep so soundly at His feet?

He is their Saviour, man and resurrected God,
And they as well must wake
And rise, with His help live more fully:
They must shake off frailty
And discard defeat.

Portrait of a Tenant

I see she's put the snail-killer down today,
The small, green pellets nestling in neat lines
Like the excreta of some exotic animal.

She recently completed another regimen:
Swept up daily
The Illawarra flame tree's fallen flowers that lay
Almost indelibly on the concrete drive
Like a scarlet paint-stain or tossed silk sheet.
She collected them meticulously,
A martyr to the cause
Of clean driveways for other's cars;
So used her empty days. With brush and pan
She shovelled them into the incinerator,
Till flame met flower
And turned it into ash.

These summer afternoons she may appear
Briefly in the garden to water, pull a weed or two,
In coat and scarf, gaunt anglophile,
Dressed against the summer's heat.

Early weekend mornings when I'm still in bed,
I've heard her moving down the sunless southern wall.
A prisoner without manacle or ball,
A heavy, joyless tread
And I wonder where it all went wrong for her.

Did she ever burn for life –
Was the candle ever lit?
Was the inner living flame somehow turned back
Or was she ravaged or consumed by it –
What fires, if any formed her?

One summer night I glimpsed her
Through her open blinds,
Dozing on her solitary bed, legs thin, pale;
Over-crossed, stark in the lamplight:
Another lonely tenant in the full-mooned night
Waiting on the final settlement.

Night on Mt Erica

Among ferns and mountain ash, lissome
Trunks, olive, cream; blazed
Bronze and indigo: this great diagonal, cantilevered
Rock
Beside the track,
Balanced on two lesser tors, roofs dusty floor
And sheltering place behind my back,
Where 200 years ago, or more:
Dark, fur-clad shapes squatted, rubbed hands,
Stamped feet, swapped tales, trivia, bemoaned
The cold; moved closer to the fire, turning away
From winds as cool and whipping now as this
Which rakes the darkening mountain side.
I sit willing myself to stillness, waiting to hear
Some echoing call across the gulf of time,
Some residue left printed on the wind;
Something to lend
This fiction I contend
Palpable weight and form. But I can decipher nothing
And now night comes on –
The track is harder to make out,
Above the gum trees' plunging crowns, clouds scud –
Moon's outriders – across the star-blown sky
As I move down the mountainside.
But sometimes a falling branch, a cracking twig
Has me glancing back.

What eyes are watching? I half expect
Some shape to rear before me on the track –
Some tentative or furious spirit of the place,
Shadowing me through it's territory –
For shadows move and shapes seem mobile
In this riot of wind and clamouring night.
I gain the car park, the key,
Warm from my pocket, fits the lock.
Green dashboard instruments light up,
Needles flicker and I read the gauges off:
Motor kicks, car rolls down forest track,
The mountain's looming silhouette recedes.

Life-drawing Model

Were your eyes blue or brown –
Blonde girl in your prime? I've known
Faces; yours was lovely.
Almond eyes professionally avoiding mine
As studiously I set myself to form, outline
Your sculpted, gold and seamless body.

Flaxen hair gathered in a small pony-tail,
Some wisps escaping. A hibiscus, sparkling green
And scarlet nestled on your neck.
Gold aubergines your breasts,
Tipped with rubies.

Like some archetypal beauty, you posed motionless,
As some model may have sat for Caravaggio –
Yet stripped of all shadow.
Maidenhair tight-curled, silvery violet,
A delicately hirsute screen over an angel's garden.

I could draw you forever and still
Not render your beauty.

Poetess Meets Poet

They met as I recall
At one of the better gatherings of the arty set.
The pictures on the wall
Were fair to middling; shiraz flowed, champagne
Was bubbling. Stuffed olives circulated on a platter
And as at all such happenings after the speeches,
Art went second fiddling.
The pictures ceased to matter:
Obscured beyond the cigarette smoke and the social chatter.

The next day for three hours,
They passed their souls' calligraphy
Across the table of an eating house in Gertrude Street –
For prearranged they'd brought their recent work.
Here, small bright coloured cups
Of coffee in the Macedonian style
Clink upon the marble tabletops.
They sipped liqueurs, clear, viscous and astringent
That left their fingers sticky, and the sun
Striking the glasses' fingerprinted sides,
Spun spectrums through the smears and globules.
Cigarettes spilled among the manuscripts.
They were lavish in each other's praise.

In minutes they'd confirmed what they already knew
About each other; their common bond was poetry.
Poetess had found Dionysian brother: he,
A sister sufferer
Of the same ecstasy.

Hamlet in Suburbia

Part of a pattern now, abandoning
A decision thought previously worthwhile,
He rolls another cigarette and slumps
Into the cerise armchair by the hissing fire
Whose bland susurrus underscores his meditations.

Beyond venetian slats, on the patio
Near wrought-iron bars, the giant green lily leaves curl back,
Stirring a little in the desultory wind.
The villa's colour scheme – white trim, blue guttering –
Is echoed in the vacuous sky
And phalanxed storm clouds slow manoeuvring

An insular, sterile suburb with few sounds of life,
Few footfalls or voices from the empty streets.
Here life is measured by a banging door,
The whining of some tethered animal.
At night the traffic's distant tide retreats
Down fog-bound hills and labyrinthine ways.

In this suburban villa, his capacity
For poor decision-making seems advanced.
He's in suspension, living in the void;
He's Hamlet's ghost, wandering unseeing down these corridors.
Turn a corner, flick a switch and face this mirror:
Who is this pitiable ogre
With such a strong desire for calm and beauty?

Refugees

Friday afternoon; after a week of teaching
English to these refugees, they and I sip coffee.
Someone's put a tape on –
'Blowing in the Wind', 'Five Hundred Miles'
And I'm surprised how these old songs
I'd thought museum pieces from an era gone,
Already history; attract them and elicit
A willingness they rarely show with my linguistic ploys
And strategies. And how these songs
Which tell of grief at parting, separation,
Passionate hope for peace in face of war,
Still hold sweet sadness in them.

'How many times must the cannon alls fly?
Lord, I'm five hundred miles from home…'
They are as intimately apprised of this
As though by fire, identifying literally:
They look out from the wreckage of their lives,
Clutching scraps of culture and identity,
Clinging to their Medusan rafts
And waiting for a phoenix to arise.

Is it only for themselves they sing, tap, hum?
Is it for them only the songs have worked an exorcism?
They are refugees form family and home,
And I from reason, probity.

All who suffer
Some dislocation at the source,
Diminishment of birthright, fatal flaw
Are refugees,
Perhaps one day we'll go home.

The Outsider

for Vincent Van Gogh

I Icons

Vincent, patron saint of artists, 'Painting is a faith',
You said. Your room at Arles, the empty chair
And pipe are icons of our modern age.
We have to overlook the badly coloured reproductions
In artistic, coffee-table books,
The legions of *Sunflowers* on the walls
Of a million dentist's waiting rooms.
It's not your fault we have to sidestep the stereotype,
Find fresh images of that rough-hewn work
That bristles with originality.

You were a prototype of so much in our time.
Not least the vocational circus, the string of jobs.
First the art dealer: you a dealer in the artefacts
Of others' souls? Then the bookseller, apprentice
Pastor in the Borinage, working with poor miners –
The same milieu as Lawrence – though you strode
Into it, chose conditions worse than theirs,
Gave them the clothes off your own back –
A saintly act, and yet you got the sack.
Rejected by the Church – a sanctuary for most –
You were destined to suffer
An outsider's destiny and quest for meaning.

Doubtless you were difficult to live with:
One whose prodigality lay in excesses of zeal.
That early photograph: at eighteen you have
That static, stunned, unfocused look of youth –
Inchoate, undefined; the puffiness of the fledgling,
The heavy youth pregnant with the older man.
By Paris, you'd sloughed off that youthful skin,
Loosened up your palette. In the self-portraits
There is the honed and pared down look
Of someone who was coming though:
Extended by art, troubled by existence.

II Arles

At Arles you really hit your stride,
Deciding to forget
All you'd recently learnt from the Impressionists,
Spending nearly everything on paints
And working through the long days' heat,
Fuelled only on bread and coffee; you were
You said, 'as happy as a cicada'.
Turning your back on Arles's Roman ruins,
You painted your way into the Modernist pantheon.
Like *The Sower* you had cast your seed,
With all that drawing and hard graft in Belgium.
Now ripe to paint, you reaped
Gold canvases from summer fields.

III The Asylum of St Paul at St Remy

He checked himself into *St Paul Hospital*, St Remy
Seeking sanctuary from a difficult world.
This was a monastic life, painting
Without the old demons of tobacco and alcohol,
But with the demon of derangement at the gates,
Held in check by constant painting.
And then his tour de force, he painted *Starry Night*
From observation, memory:
Great, cartwheeling stars, effulgent flashlights,
Thread the purple sky above the sleeping town.
A dark cypress to the left pencils upward
To the highest stars; the church's steeple to the right
Sticks up like an antenna,
As if to channel that electric energy
That crackles through the mountains, stars and trees.
Van Gogh with his circular, twisting forms and snaking line,
Has painted symbols of the infinite, the divine:
His own idiosyncratic pantheism.

Odalisque

After *La Grande Odalisque* by Jean-Auguste-Dominique Ingres

Once we sat by the sea wall
Under the full moon,
Watching the silver waves
Come sliding in, the sea's caress.
You an enigma, tall
In your 60s fashion,
Multicoloured, sheath of a dress.

Forty years ago, a whole lifetime away,
I tried to prise your identity from you
With intrusive, well-meaning questions.

Now your face turns to me
Over the cool flesh of your shoulder,
Your gaze knowing, yet restrained;
The long line of your back curves
To the hip
Then disappears discreetly
Into these silken sheets.

Now, I know you:
Svelte, tall and elegant,
Neither Earth Mother nor Madonna,
But archetypal courtesan.

If only we'd found such a suitable love-nest,
Hung around with these sumptuous silks.
If only I'd been able to charm you
Out of your garments!

There you are.
Gazing out of this picture,
Holding the whisk of peacock feathers
Close to your thigh.

The Minoans

The first true civilisation,
The Minoans were a gentle, genial people;
Merchants and traders, skilled artisans; but above all artists
Of the bull-leaping, seen in palace murals.
Brave youths and maidens, grasping the bull's horns,
Somersaulting over the beast's back,
With great courage, skill and joie de vivre:
The bull was not killed – unlike in other cultures –
Being a symbol of nature and male potency.

According to the records, they fought no wars,
Built great palaces with modern plumbing,
But did not bother to build walls
To fortify their island against intruders –
The Mycenaeans: tall, bearded, grim, a warrior race –
To the Minoans, slender, youthful, open hearted,
The Mycenaeans were always going to be a problem.

They worshipped the Snake Goddess
In little effigies of faience*
Placed in shrines in homes and palaces.
She is young, approachable, with a leopard on her head –
A symbol of her command of nature's wild forces.
She holds a snake in each fist,
Wears a full flounced skirt with elaborate stomacher†
Pushing forth bared breasts.
She is unlike the gods of other cultures:
Egypt, Assyria, Sumer.

* faience – decorated earthenware, porcelain
† stomacher – women's article of dress worn, in this case, from beneath the breasts to the pit of the stomach

There was a golden age, then the Mycenaeans slowly
Strangled their trade routes,
Wore down their resistance; the coup de grace came
When Santorini exploded, sending ash and tidal waves
Over the island.
Later, Crete was settled and ruled by others,
The Minoans vanished into history.

Leaves

for Meredith

Quiet installations sucked heat from the air,
Waiters moved behind your chair,
And once, when the green leaves shimmered
Beyond the high, cool sheets of glass
That rose behind you there –
Leaves heaped like a vertical sea,
Each soft furl of foliage a billow,
Each trembling, white bellied leaf
A shifting myriad of surface making –

Then, I looked a second longer
In your lidded eyes – you had painted lines
On your lids as a Chinese painter may
Have brushed twin crescents onto parchment –

Perceiving there something bringing my mind
Up sharp:
Sheer, clear, abrupt
Like the pane of window glass.
And I, a wayward mariner,
Was out of my depth
And seeking shelter

In those evanescent, shifting planes of green
Leaves shimmering, each over the other sliding,
Softly embattled, heaped and beckoning:
And I was lost, no charts
In those cool, green seas of your eyes.

Rough-edged Voices

I love those voices
That talk when they sing,
Sing when they talk,
Whose music is tangible.

Voices that weave
An antique, brilliant fabric:
Renbourn and Jansch, Clannad,
Bensusan, Stivell;
Diamonds and motley.
Music with a rough husk,
Sweet immanence.

Voices which inhabit
That shadowland
Of harmony and dissonance:
Dylan and Faithfull,
Voices which possess
A bitter-sweet ambivalence.

I love those voices with rough edges,
Not the 'smooth 'n' easy' singers.
'Some of the people can be part right some of the time,
All of the people can be part right all of the time,
But all of the people can't be all right all of the time.'
I think Abraham Lincoln said that.

It is easier for a Kamahl or a Humperdink
To pass through the eye of a needle
Than it is for their music to please me.
And I know that the voice of a true singer
Comes from the Kingdom of Heaven:
I said that.

Out of the Clamour

You came to my table out of the clamour of that place
And utterly transformed the day,
And following days also
Could never again be the same
After your coming.
You had sown grain, which putting out shoots,
Put out leaves
Whose shadows have altered the ensuing days.

I, who have sought you amongst the usual faces,
Have failed in the finding.
For I have sought you with my dark and lesser self,
Our meetings have remained
Unresolved and fleeting,
And there has fallen
A kind of a shadow across our relations.

I wish you would return to my table;
That I once again may find you
Entire in myself and whole.

Last Year at Marienbad

After the film by Alain Resnais

These passages without end, corridors stretching interminably.
Walls of black marble, aspidistra, hushed colloquies
At chess or at cards, salons silent, yet peopled.
Ornate mirrors return illusion to illusion.
Staircases spiral to space only,
As if in etchings by Piranesi.
Time is irrelevant
In airless boudoirs where lovers are suspended
In soliloquy; rooms costive with dust and inaction.

The gardens laid out like a progression of logarithms.
All here is hiatus, an ambience of stasis.
A place of endless, labyrinthine passages,
The architectural incarnation of monotonous
And perpetual repetition.

What is this passionless and enervated space –
This silent purgatorial place?

Suburban Adieux

'Goodnight!' The car doors thud,
The motor revs, the guests recede
In the machine. She turns,
Hardly aware of her companion,
Who galvanised to action by routine,
Coils down the hose, throws the anti-prowler switch
On the Cyclone palisade
And garages the family limousine.

Her brocade high heels pock the red, swept gravel
Of this meticulously kept domain,
Over which the broad back of her attentive husband,
A capable man,
Casts a frenetic shadow.

Lines on a Photo of Bob Dylan, c. 1966

There you stand, unblinking in the sun, more than
A little dazed, uncharacteristically
Without the shades – but they're there anyway
In the folded hands with the ubiquitous cigarette.
And I wonder which of those extraordinary
Ground-breaking records you were working on
The day they took that photograph.
The suede jacket and the hair suggest
It might be 'Blonde on Blonde',
With its swirling organ and that 'high, wild
Mercury sound of thin metallic gold'.

How different this appearance to '62's
Close-cropped, serious singer of austere protest
Songs and earnest anthems.
Here, there is something of the decadent,
Elegant heir to Baudelaire: a minimalist 60s dandy,
Neo-romantic rock-urchin. Chameleon poet,

How often have you sung in a new style,
New idiom? You not only irrevocably changed
The popular song, bringing it a new complexity,
But changed the way a generation thought
About itself.

Now you have seen the departures
Of some of your confrères – Harrison, Petty, Ginsberg
Have all shuffled off the scene –
You must feel more than a little mortal.
But then every day for you could still be a New Morning.
You are the Shakespeare of our times.
What riches might you strew before us yet?

On the Death of Anna Magdalena Bach

Not just his inspiratrix, amanuensis, copyist,
An accomplished keyboard player,
She was her own woman.
Not to mention the extraordinary feat of bearing
Thirteen surviving children by the age of forty,
Clearly a woman of profound resources.

Her last years lacked the accomplishments of her first.
After Bach's death, she lived in poverty, extraordinarily
Neglected by her many children.
Dying at 58, laid in an unmarked grave in Leipzig,
The final indignity came in World War II:
The Allies bombed her grave to smithereens.

Nothing physical remains.
Yet she is still with us in her hidden legacy.
Without her skills, how would he achieve?
Without her strength, how was he sustained?
Without her body, how would live exist?
There is no final resting place.
Her spirit shimmers somewhere out there in the ether:
A generous, loving soul who gave her all,
Spurned by progeny and fate.

Woman, Sea and Myth

No surprise that myth has woman rising
From the sea.
The white or ochre sand, her warm body,
The waves the colour of her eyes –
All weathers give all shades –
And salt for her tears.

If you still doubt then look at Botticelli.
I'm sure he fashioned Aphrodite's hair
On those great wet skeins of brown and yellow kelp
You see enmeshed with sea berries
Washed up on the shore.

Pearl and shells her toe and finger nails,
And let sharp coral be
The reefs where all her hapless victims founder.
Let tracery
Of nerve and deep desire
And shadowed ebb and flow of feeling be
The sea-swung sea fern, sea bush and anemone.

Storm After Calm

Onshore wind and a light rain mist-driven,
Gulls plane overhead or stand: mute groups
In the shore's lea. Further down where the wind's bleaker,
Each grey-green breaker lifts and crashes.

Only the mono-sails of a few windsurfers,
Stained glass slivers
Tumble in the bay's kaleidoscope
Beyond in the dusk, slow car lights climb and descend
The mauve spiral of Westgate
Near the stack of the powerhouse at Newport.

Monday, and a sea change
After heat's lassitude, sky's blue vacancy;
The press and assortment of glistening bodies,
Cacophony of shared music: ersatz repose.
The weekend's relentless and passive pursuit of pleasure

Cannot better this peace by wind fractured,
Air wet but mobile.
From leaden clouds edged with copper,
Spokes of sunlight stall over the bay.
In the white distance: beach-bins daubed pastel
Lemon, pale blue, green, red lean awry
Down the blown sand's vista.
A distant figure in orange
Crosses the sand to the water.

Burke and Wills at Cooper Creek

1860, Royal Park, Melbourne. The cavalcade leaves
Via Essendon to Menindee, weaving its way
Across an empty map
To camp at Cooper Creek.

Here the base camp party waits three months
As the four lunge for the Gulf.
Depleted, they stumble back to find
The camp deserted:
The base-camp party headed south that very day.

Longstaff's painting: dejection personified and doom.
The exhausted explorers standing in the gloom.
The tree marked DIG9ftW* –
The ground just newly broken:
The message read, supplies dislodged,
Few words are spoken. They are as alone
As if stranded on that very moon
That hangs there full, behind the drooping eucalypt.

Burke: a gung-ho Anglocentric, stubborn Irish cop,
An adventurer from Bendigo with something to prove;
An opera prima donna for his love –
A curious cove
To lead a well-heeled expedition
Into the interior's cold and fiery heart.
And Wills: the recorder, diarist, sound
And careful surveyor of all they won and lost;
The thinker to Burke's blusterer, the measurer,
The counter of the cost.
Yet perhaps too cautious.

Did he ever argue with his leader, seek
To get some of those decisions turned around?
How many fatal decisions can one man make?
Did he ever grab Burke by the shoulders, try to shake
Some sense into him – or influence him to take
Some decisions for the expedition's sake?

So, at Burke's command, they struck out west
Into the desert for the shimmering mirage
Of Mt Hopeless (if ever there was an omen),
Rather than take the guaranteed, southbound, homing track.
The heat flowed round them in waves,
Red dust in eyes and mouths,
Food and water low.
The desultory clack and skid of sharp stones
On blistered feet.
They were driven back in pitiful retreat
To Cooper Creek.

To languish beside heat-depleted waterholes,
To lie in a state of limbo, awaiting a rescue
That would come too late.
Hearing the raucous cries of cockatoos
At dusk. Seeing with fading sight the flitting shapes
Of the blacks, who would have brought them food and water
Had not Burke waved his revolver, raged and blustered.

---

* Dig nine feet west: a cache of food and provisions

Meditation on the Past while Swimming: A Tale of Two Countries

I

Swimming laps, I ask myself
Why couldn't I have done this at 16, 17?
Exploded out of that dumb cycle of paralysis,
That narcissistic vortex into which I sank:
A kind of whirlpool of the soul and mind,
When most days had a sinking feeling
And with nothing firm beneath my feet,
I struggled for control.

II

Would it have helped at all
To have had those gold, antipodean beaches then,
That hard, clear southern light?
Some chlorine-drenched Olympic pool in a country town,
To somehow bleach away and cleanse
That dank neurosis, that miasma of the soul
That hung about me over in that northern land
Where I could count my swimming forays on one hand?

III

Life here would have been more physical,
More chance of gaining 'in-pool prowess',
Tasting the lotus eaters' drugs of surf and sun.
Instead, I gained keen apprehension
Of that watery English light
Captured by Constable and Bonnington;
Memories of idyllic fields, where in the shade
I propped my bike and saw the shimmering
Spires of Oxford through the summer haze.
The purple shadows and the leafy ways
Of Regent's Park Canal…

Song for Miriam

I watch the new spring's lovers mingle,
I walk alone beneath dark trees;
I seems that only I walk single,
Feeling the loss of other days than these,

When you and I walked clinging,
Spellbound in each other's gaze;
Your eyes shining, my mind singing
Songs of love down gold, autumnal ways.

When you and I went wandering
Through the purple, neoned night,
Over face-thronged, glistening pavements,
Dual minds charged with multi-coloured light.

When you and I my love, were loving
Travellers in each other's arms;
Giving, taking honied kisses,
Conjuring love with Aphrodite's charms.

Now memory's image, etched with acid,
You sit framed inside that door,
Seemingly not with the others.
I came to you across the floor.

It wasn't chance that led me to you,
No accidental boy–girl glance,
I already knew I knew you
As I took your hand to lead you from that dance.

But gentle days don't last forever,
The omniscient author of the cosmic song,
Assigned us short scenes in life's drama:
The highest pitch can't be maintained for long.

I watch these new spring lovers mingle,
I walk these parkland paths alone.
I find the seat we kissed and talked on
The night I walked you through the darkness to your home,

When you and I began our loving
Underneath the vast, starred skies;
Rustling lamplit leaves above us
Danced dappled light across your lidded eyes.

The last time you and I were loving,
You came naked up to me;
Fresh from bathing, white and glistening,
Like Venus rising from a silver sea.

Here, fresh mauve flowers recall your beauty,
Green plants shoot from moist, tilled earth.
I thank the gods for you my lady,
For having brought this love of ours to birth.

Now, I don't like the way the wind blows,
I'll try to curb my mind's unease;
Then I'll go the way my heart knows:
To you and better days than these.

Ballade

for Phillada

I sat down in Hampstead town
With a girl with lemon hair.
I had a friend called Dominic
And he was with us there.

We had spent the afternoon
Wandering over Hampstead Heath.
I had climbed an old dead tree,
Looked down laughing at her face beneath.

I had taken her green shoes
And hidden them beneath the tree.
I stood there watching her blue eyes laughing
As she waved the shoes at me.

Then she took off her rainbow cape,
And spread it on the ground,
Then we sang songs to an old guitar;
The woods gave back the sound.

And once at home, with shining eyes,
She held mine captive in her stare.
The day had gone, what had I done
To earn this Venus with the lemon hair?

Bibliomaiden

Our meetings at first were tentative,
Timorous, uncertain. We would meet
Always in the same location,
Under the great dome, near the green lights in the gloom.
Oblivious, yet aware of strange shadows,
Scuttling, muttering in the semi-dark –
Drab-coated, hunched little men, always hatted
Scanned legal volumes, tirelessly seeking
Legal loopholes to a strangling marriage.

But our brief, intense and emphatic assignations
Would commence identically: I would present
A little ticket with your name and number to your warders,
Who would scrutinise the billet briefly,
Vanish quietly, commandeer you
From some high, remote and silent chamber.
And I nervously waiting below for you,
Would start when they announced you,
Claim you self-consciously,
Carry you off to our trysting.

Oh, you were no dog-eared library whore,
(But you were no virgin),
Slim, green and elegant
From your last lover you came,
Bibliomaiden.

Neither was I uxorious; I did not buy you,
Nor set you upon my shelf.
You were destined to be
Both enjoyed and enhanced
By an anthology of selected lovers –
I, one among them.

Gradually our meetings were easier,
We grew used to each other.
You flowed toward me, holding back nothing:
We devoured one another.

Yet I knew even then, that our meetings were numbered –
You had given your all to me,
I would read you no further.

Go then. But as you lie in your high, remote chamber,
Awaiting the summons of your next admirer,
Let us both not fail to remember

Our so well regulated,
Quietly satisfying and seductive meetings,
When under the great dome, near the green lights
In the gloom and the flickering shadows,
I was your bibliolover
And you were my bibliomaiden.

In the Reading Room of the State Library of Victoria

Marine Vignette

Illuminated by a Persian moon
Like the Copenhagen maid upon her rock, you sat.
The silent, teeming ocean seemed a wind-stirred arras
Hung up behind this painter's dream.
Silver dolphins thronged
Black velvet, corrugating waves,
Which rose in crests of splintered foam.

Some fashionable gold and purple-patterned robe
The wind compressed in ripples
Round about you. While within your aura
Charged by reverie, the sea air seemed to vibrate palpably:
As though you sat in some electric field
Fed by the battery of the night.

Thoughts of an Educator

Some of them still seem young enough to play
By the sea where the small waves lap,
Others older skip and play in the shallows,
Some swim close to the shore.
They do not hear me
Calling to them

Treading water,
Over the abyss.

By the Pool: A Summer Poem

Approaching the pool's exit turn-style,
Chlorine fumes rising from damp concrete in the heat,
I view a large, recumbent female body,
Reclining face-down, on a pool-side banana lounge.

Hot sun beats down on creamy skin and golden hair
Done up in a chignon. She's certainly substantial –
You might say 'Rubensesque' – or even possessing
The proportions of a sculpture by Henry Moore.
I hesitate to think, 'beached whale' –
That would be unkind.
But what really exercises my voyeuristic mind
Is this: I assume I'm surveying the torso
Of a thirty- or forty-year-old…

Passing, I turn, seeking her face
And am utterly surprised to behold the visage
Of a sixteen-year-old girl intent on a Maeve Binchy novel.
Exiting, I consider
This strangely disturbing phenomenon: the conjunction
Of a young girl's head
On the massive body of a mature woman

A Cinnamon Girl in Cosmos Book Store

I'm listening to a CD, propped on a stool, abstracted…
The brown, honeyish woman, first I see her
Smooth, strong legs, tailored navy shorts,
Full curve of calf from just behind the knee,
Near ebony. Hair dark, easy curls, not crisp,
Just shoulder length.

Brown good looks,
The sweet smile she shot
At the girl assistant. She had a line
About her, a clear-eyed sensuality:
Strong, brown, stimulating –
Coffee without the sugar.

The curve of calf behind the knee,
Implying other curves,
Full, brown…
Lying on her belly in some dim-lit room,
On a hot day after love-making; bands of light
Through the wood-slat blinds,
On white, crumpled sheets.
And in front: not too pilose, but a short-cropped sweet
Patch aromatic; lowering your eyes,
The dark delta would become a world:
Musk, incense and patchouli,
The salt taste of her tides.

Cricket Ground, Walhalla

First, steps: we climb the rough track,
Grey rocks jut
From red, clay base: a long, scooped incline
Veering up to this scalped, levelled hilltop.
Dry grass stretches away –
We stare across the lens-like field
To gums as if painted by Glover.
Their sapphire foliage still –
Mute spectators on the boundary.
Wind-riffled seed-ears nod
On bleached straw stems.
This great, silent disc seeded by air and light:
A place to pause, meditate, assess.

Peering into an obscure arena, an amphitheatre
Of the mind and heart:
To look backwards to what was,
To dismiss what have might have been.
This quiet field, a lens
Up to which we hold our actions for inspection –

Or some great sieve, which we could shake
To separate our acts' impurities out:
Discard the dross
And keep the finest gold.

Walhalla is a disused gold-mining town in East Gippsland, Victoria.

Bob Dylan at Budokan

Tambourine Man with your white mask on,
At Budokan tonight you sing, take liberties
With your own legendary songs; syncopate, change
Phrases, harmonies. You are before a crowd
You do not know, who don't know you
And I have never heard you sound so easy, light and lyrical.
Up there you're all alone – I've read
That's how you like it, that's your choice.
Before a 'Simple Twist of Fate', that gravel voice
Is soft, almost confessional: the stress on '*Here's*
A simple love story…'
All this is new:

The music's lighter, though still tight and tough –
Like tinkling bells or pattering rain.
The brass is strident only to be sweet.
There's no strain in your voice –
I've heard you roar our rough –
And some old classics have a reggae beat.
Between the songs it's 'Thank you,
'See if you can guess this one!'
Tonight you are not stranded on your feet,
Nor is there any darkness in your mind.

A masked magician on electric lute,
You lay down the opening bars,
The silver saxophones begin to play,
While you transmute some raw incident
Into the realm of myth:
And once again you sing
That same old story of lost love
In an entirely different way.

Viewing John Olsen's Pictures at the National Gallery of Victoria

'A sort of wild freedom, the curtain of appearances ruffled by the wind of insight'

I

Outside, the gallery walls, monotonous and sheer
Say something about what's inside –
How austerity can speak of promise,
How mere appearances
Can hide rich plenitude.

II

The animals are approachable.
Ethereal, small owlets floating in the paint's grey plasma.
Ebullient elephants squirt blue water,
Frolic in depths of emerald joy.
Giraffes, elastic necks, loll yo-yo tongues
From rubbery lips. At Bungle Bungle, camel humps:
Filmy outgrowths from red, blotched earth.

III

A child plays by the sea, blue-bottles, old shoes;
Acidic yellow lines and light; the vast sides
Of a ship, purple, oxidic red slide by.
Five bells ring out
As Joe Lynch, beer bottles in pockets, plummets
Like a stone through moon-shafted waters.*
Little wheels of thought clicking in the purple deep:
The siren city dances upside-down.

IV

Velasquez's fried egg sizzles in the gloom,
Don Quixote wanders in past Renoir's laid-out brushes,
El Amoladar lurches down La Calle Estrecha
In yellows and reds, all manner of paraphernalia clattering.
Degas stares from collapsed eyes out
Into the street, where Becket joins the gypsy caravan.

V

Outside, my feet lift lighter;
The fountains echo in their shapes
The camel's necks and humps.
My brain floats up again into my Lake Eyre skull.

Some local knowledge: Joe Lynch, a passenger on a cross-harbour ferry, fell overboard and, owing to his weighted pockets, quickly sank.

Varykino Lost

After *Doctor Zhivago* by Boris Pasternak

After the long journey, the Zhivagos came to Varykino
Finding it waiting; good omens everywhere,
Despite the boy Sasha's tired screaming.
The wall-length window giving onto space,
The distant carpet of diminutive pine,
The talk with Gromeko, under the stars' bright ceiling.
The women pouring tea and the friendly conversation
Of the Mikulitsuns, despite their brusque greeting.

And the small, abandoned annexe which became their home,
Hidden by nettles on the old estate.
They spent that spring and summer in feverish refurbishment
For their first winter at Varykino.

Here in solitude, Zhivago turned again
To his diary, his forgotten poems, meditations on art
And literature; talking Tolstoy, Dostoievsky, Pushkin's
Onegin with Samdevyatov till early morning.

Then, in Yuryatin at the library,
He looked up to see
Her head bent uncoquettishly over her reading.
He declined a second look. His guttering mind flared up
Then steadied like a flame:
He worked again, transmuted, on his book.

They were lovers. He rode from Varykino often to see her
Opposite the House of the Caryatids; the cool light
Of her northern beauty in the unlit door,
The unowned gift of her whiteness gleaming before him.

Then that last evening, rushing to get home,
The sun in gold bars through the birch branches,
The half-heard shots, a forest crossroads;
The three stern horsemen, the abduction in sudden confusion,

The shifting darkness. The paradise of Varykino
Suddenly like a carpet, unmagically swept from beneath him.

Muirstead

At Muirstead, Portland, Victoria

I

At thirty yards the gum trees stand, a shifting screen
Changing in moments with the differing wind,
In texture with a sudden fall of light;
Like the façade that Monet watched for days at Rouen.
Here, it seems I am the sole observer,
Actor, critic in this play
Of light and solitude, where kookaburras plane
In silent arcs across this backdrop
To the whitewashed paling fence, pale blue gate
And gay nasturtiums nearer to the house.

II

The interior could be the cabin of pioneers –
Those men who opened up this land with Dutton,
Henty, then moved up the Wannon.
The frypan on the open stove, the red firebricks,
The blocks of yellow gum. Electric light,
The automatic fridge, the telephone
All seem superfluous necessities.
Gas lamps have in fact
Shed the aura of their hissing light
On winter nights here at Bolwara;
Within these darkly panelled walls,
Creating a chiaroscuro out of modern time.

III

Along the winding track, hidden in luxuriant bush,
Past indolent retreating snakes
And purple, flowering vine:
The lonely reality of a Wyeth shack.
Hidden among trees and fallow fields
And northern pine; and in the middle distance
Up behind the house, an ever-moving stand of forest gum
Above which I've seen the predatory eagle fly
Then vanish on the wind.
With scattered outhouses of grey wood
And straggling, red gravel paths;
A leaning garage freshly painted blue,
Tilted at a crazy angle to the sky.
Mauve-white berries by the dunny door,
A kitchen garden greenly run to seed,
The sun-bleached palings sagging at the back.
To such solitude as this Zhivago might have come
To till the soil, to write the journal of his soul,
To rest his bones and gaze at nightfall
At the lanterns of the stars.

IV

The poem is made, the day is put aside.
The moon so full, so luminous
It obliterates the stars.
Only Orion is salient
Above an inky streak of cypress, darkly green;
Only the fence wire's dewy sheen
Scored silver on the fencepost's shadowed vertebrae.
The moonlight drips like candlewax across the landscape.

Candle in the Wind

This candle-flame is played with
By the warm night's wind,
Is lengthened out and like a streamer strung;
Then battered downward to the horizontal
And small compressed into a golden tongue.

I sit here at this darkened table –
The Nocturnes from an inner room –
Utterly perplexed at how to handle
This dark unmitigated all-pervading gloom
That penetrates and hangs about me
And must to others label me a man of doom.

Life to me seems like that candle;
Each day the guttering flame
Spun round in nerves' hot wind,
Ever flickering, swinging, fluttering –
Not still and steady; and I pray
This flame of mine may find a quieter way to glow,
That I am not yet ready to burn out.

Your Gypsy Dress

It slipped off your full
shoulders, fell from
your famous arms,
sluiced your
brown buds
of nipples
and fell
like
rainbowed
water easily
over slender waist
and solid thighs –
their rich dark
triangle of
delight:
to lie
like rippling, light-flashed water around your
naked feet.

www.ingramcontent.com/pod-product-compliance
Lightning Source LLC
Chambersburg PA
CBHW070331120526
44590CB00017B/2847